RHODE ISLAND

The Ocean State

BY
JOHN HAMILTON

Abdo & Daughters
An imprint of Abdo Publishing | abdopublishing.com

Published by ABDO Publishing, a division of ABDO, PO Box 398166, Minneapolis, Minnesota 55439. Copyright © 2017 by Abdo Consulting Group, Inc. International copyrights reserved in all countries. No part of this book may be reproduced in any form without written permission from the publisher. ABDO & Daughters™ is a trademark and logo of ABDO Publishing.

Printed in the United States of America, North Mankato, Minnesota.
062016
092016

THIS BOOK CONTAINS
RECYCLED MATERIALS

Editor: Sue Hamilton   **Contributing Editor:** Bridget O'Brien
Graphic Design: Sue Hamilton
Cover Art Direction: Candice Keimig   **Cover Photo Selection:** Neil Klinepier
Cover Photo: iStock
Interior Images: Alamy, America's Cup Event Authority, AP, Arthur's Cooking, Big Blue Bug Solutions, Brown University Bears, Bryant University Bulldogs, Dreamstime, Getty, Glow Images, Granger Collection, Hasbro, iStock, History in Full Color-Restoration/Colorization, Library of Congress, Mile High Maps, Mountain High Maps, One Mile Up, Paul Carrick, Pawtucket Red Sox, Providence Bruins, Providence Friers, RhodeIsland.gov, Shutterstock, University of Rhode Island Rams, University of Wisconsin Milwaukee, & Wikimedia.

Statistics: *State and City Populations*, U.S. Census Bureau, July 1, 2015 estimates; *Land and Water Area*, U.S. Census Bureau, 2010 Census, MAF/TIGER database; *State Temperature Extremes*, NOAA National Climatic Data Center; *Climatology and Average Annual Precipitation*, NOAA National Climatic Data Center, 1980-2015 statewide averages; *State Highest and Lowest Points*, NOAA National Geodetic Survey.

Websites: To learn more about the United States, visit booklinks.abdopublishing.com. These links are routinely monitored and updated to provide the most current information available.

Cataloging-in-Publication Data

Names: Hamilton, John, 1959- author.
Title: Rhode Island / by John Hamilton.
Description: Minneapolis, MN : Abdo Publishing, [2017] | Series: The United
     States of America | Includes index.
Identifiers: LCCN 2015957731 | ISBN 9781680783421 (lib. bdg.) |
     ISBN 9781680774467 (ebook)
Subjects: LCSH: Rhode Island--Juvenile literature.
Classification: DDC 974.5--dc23
LC record available at http://lccn.loc.gov/2015957731

CONTENTS

THE OCEAN STATE

Rhode Island is the smallest state in the Union, but only when measured in square miles. It is big in many other ways. It is a densely populated powerhouse with a good economy and plenty of natural beauty. Rhode Island has much to offer visitors and residents alike.

One of the original 13 colonies, Rhode Island is part of New England. It lies along the East Coast of the United States. Its independent-minded people work hard, but they also know how to have fun. Some of their favorite things to do include fishing, boating, or swimming along the state's many beaches and waterways.

Rhode Island has nearly 400 miles (644 km) of coastline. State residents are never more than a 30-minute drive from the Atlantic Ocean or the sparkling waters of Narragansett Bay. That is why Rhode Island is called "The Ocean State."

A statue of Roger Williams overlooks Providence, Rhode Island. Williams founded the city in 1636, hoping to create a place with religious and political freedom.

Castle Hill Lighthouse aids ship traffic bound for Newport or Providence, Rhode Island, via the East Passage of Narragansett Bay.

QUICK FACTS

Name: Origin uncertain. Dutch explorer Adriaen Block called Aquidneck Island (where the first colony was established) *Roodt Eylandt* (Red Island), perhaps because of the color of its clay soil. Another explorer, Giovanni de Verrazzano, said it reminded him of the Greek island of Rhodes.

State Capital: Providence, population 179,207

Date of Statehood: May 29, 1790 (13th state)

Population: 1,056,298 (43rd-most populous state)

Area (Total Land and Water): 1,545 square miles (4,002 sq km), smallest state

Largest City: Providence, population 179,207

Nickname: The Ocean State

Motto: Hope

State Bird: Rhode Island Red Chicken

State Flower: Violet

State Rock: Cumberlandite

State Tree: Red Maple

State Song: "Rhode Island's It For Me"

Highest Point: Jerimoth Hill, 812 feet (247 m)

Lowest Point: Atlantic Ocean, 0 feet (0 m)

Average July High Temperature: 81°F (27°C)

Record High Temperature: 104°F (40°C), in Providence on August 2, 1975

Average January Low Temperature: 20°F (-7°C)

Record Low Temperature: -28°F (-33°C), in Wood River Junction on January 11, 1942

Average Annual Precipitation: 48 inches (122 cm)

Number of U.S. Senators: 2

Number of U.S. Representatives: 2

U.S. Postal Service Abbreviation: RI

GEOGRAPHY

Rhode Island is the smallest state of the United States. Its land area covers just 1,034 square miles (2,678 sq km). Bordering Rhode Island to the west is the state of Connecticut. To the north and east is Massachusetts. The Atlantic Ocean is to the south.

Rhode Island is about 37 miles (60 km) wide and 48 miles (77 km) long. However, its shoreline is approximately 400 miles (644 km) long, thanks to the winding shape of Narragansett Bay and its many islands. The bay reaches far inland from the Atlantic Ocean, nearly cutting the state in half north-to-south.

Narragansett Bay reaches far inland, nearly cutting Rhode Island in half.

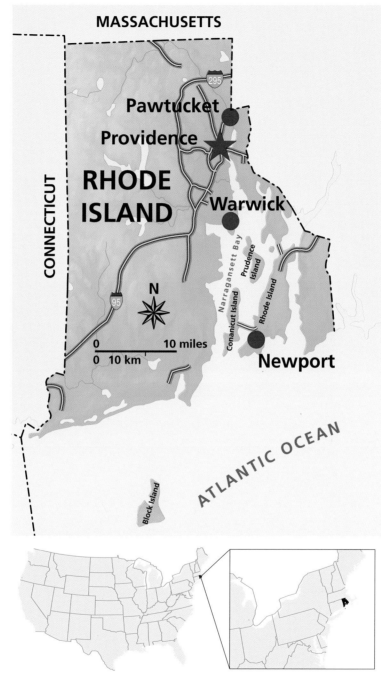

Rhode Island's total land and water area is 1,545 square miles (4,002 sq km). It is the smallest state. The state capital is Providence.

The Blackstone River flows through Rhode Island's Coastal Lowlands region.

Most of Rhode Island is flat. The highest point is Jerimoth Hill. It is in the northwestern part of the state, near the Connecticut border. It rises just 812 feet (247 m) above sea level.

There are two main land regions in Rhode Island. The western two-thirds of the state is part of the New England Upland. It is filled with rolling hills, forests, lakes, and rivers. There are many small towns and farms in this region.

The eastern third of Rhode Island is called the Coastal Lowlands region. It includes the Atlantic Ocean coast and the area surrounding Narragansett Bay, which extends northward from the ocean. Along the shoreline are salt marshes, lagoons, and sandy beaches. The Providence, Blackstone, and Pawtuxet Rivers flow through the region, emptying into Narragansett Bay.

Narragansett Bay is the largest estuary in New England. There are more than 30 islands in the bay. The largest include Aquidneck, Conanicut, and Prudence Islands.

About 13 miles (21 km) south of Rhode Island's southern shore is Block Island. It is a glacial moraine left over by Ice Age glaciers. Rhode Island was once covered by ice up to one mile (1.6 km) thick. The ice scraped and shaped the land as it crept forward. When it finally melted, about 10,000 years ago, it left behind big deposits of sand, gravel, and other rocks. Today, Block Island's sandy beaches make it a popular summer tourist spot.

Block Island's sandy beaches make it a popular tourist spot.

CLIMATE AND
WEATHER

Rhode Island is between two major climate zones: humid continental and humid subtropical. The weather is usually damp and changeable, with swings in daily and seasonal temperatures.

The state has four distinct seasons. Summers are usually hot, with plenty of rainfall. Statewide, the average high temperature in July is 81°F (27°C). The record high is 104°F (40°C), which occurred in Providence on August 2, 1975.

Storm clouds begin to build on a summer day in Rhode Island.

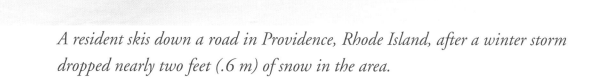

A resident skis down a road in Providence, Rhode Island, after a winter storm dropped nearly two feet (.6 m) of snow in the area.

In winter, cold temperatures and snow are likely. The average January low temperature is 20°F (-7°C). The record low happened in Wood River Junction on January 11, 1942. On that day, the thermometer sank to a teeth-chattering -28°F (-33°C).

Rhode Island is sometimes struck with severe weather, including thunderstorms in the summer and blizzards in winter. Hurricanes have also struck the state. They have whipped up storm surges measuring 18 feet (5 m) high. Storm surges can cause terrible damage and even loss of life along coastal areas. The most destructive hurricanes to strike Rhode Island in modern history include the 1938 New England Hurricane, and Hurricane Carol in 1954.

PLANTS AND
ANIMALS

Forests cover 367,885 acres (148,878 ha) of Rhode Island. That is about 56 percent of its land area. Most of the trees are deciduous, which means their leaves turn color and then fall off in the autumn. The most common tree species include red maple, white oak, northern red oak, and eastern white pine. Also found are ash, birch, cedar, hickory, and tulip trees. The official state tree of Rhode Island is the red maple. In the autumn, these shade trees turn a fiery red color.

Red Maple Tree

Rhode Island has many salt marshes. They are found in places along the Narragansett Bay estuary where saltwater from the Atlantic Ocean mixes with freshwater from rivers and streams. Growing in the salt marshes are smooth cordgrass and salt hay grasses. Healthy salt marshes control flooding, as well as filter sediments and toxins from river runoff, which helps keep Narragansett Bay clean. The marshes also shelter many kinds of wildlife, especially birds such as egrets and ducks.

White Egret

There are many kinds of wildflowers that grow in Rhode Island's forests, marshes, and meadows. They include daisies, trilliums, lilies, bloodroots, irises, and pimpernels. In the spring, the forests get a splash of color from flowering dogwoods, rhododendrons, and mountain laurels. The state flower is the violet.

The biggest animals that regularly live in Rhode Island's forests are white-tailed deer. Moose and black bears occasionally wander into the state from neighboring Massachusetts and Connecticut. Smaller animals found in Rhode Island include beavers, bobcats, coyotes, muskrats, opossums, foxes, fishers, otters, rabbits, raccoons, skunks, woodcocks, and weasels.

White-tailed deer are common in Rhode Island's forests.

Wild Turkeys

Rhode Island is a great destination for bird watchers. There are many kinds of habitats for avian species, from woodlands to pastures to marshes. Birds often spotted in the state include ducks, eagles, doves, egrets, geese, falcons, gulls, herons, loons, pheasants, ruffed grouses, sparrows, and swans. Wild turkeys have recently been reintroduced into the state after being over-hunted nearly to extinction in the early 1900s.

The state bird is the Rhode Island Red chicken. First raised and bred in the state, the hardy birds have rust-colored feathers. They are raised for meat and eggs, but are also popular show birds.

Rhode Island's saltwater and freshwater fish include striped bass, bluefish, flounder, menhaden, pickerel, pollock, scup, swordfish, tautog, and trout. Finback and humpback whales can sometimes be spotted in the Atlantic Ocean, as well as seals, dolphins, and sea turtles.

Common shellfish include clams, crabs, lobsters, oysters, and mussels. Rhode Island's state shellfish is the quahog. They are a large, tasty kind of clam.

Quahogs

PLANTS AND ANIMALS

HISTORY

People have been living in the Rhode Island area for at least 8,000 to 10,000 years. Not much is known about these Paleo-Indians, who were the distant ancestors of today's Native Americans. Only a few of their tools, such as stone spear points, have been unearthed by archeologists.

By the time Europeans first arrived in Rhode Island in the early 1500s, several groups of Native Americans had formed in the area. The tribes included the Wampanoag, Pequot, Narragansett, and Nipmuck peoples. They hunted, fished, and grew crops such as corn and beans.

A statue of Massasoit, a leader of the Wampanoag tribe. He and his people lived in today's Warren, Rhode Island.

Roger Williams arrived in Rhode Island in 1636. He and other settlers bought land from the Narragansett Native Americans and started the city of Providence.

In 1524, Italian Giovanni de Verrazzano became the first European to explore the Rhode Island coast, including Narragansett Bay and Block Island. He was looking for a sea route to China, which he never found. In 1614, Dutch sailor Adriaen Block also explored the area.

Rhode Island's first permanent European settlement was built in 1636. English Puritan Roger Williams came to the area after being banished from Massachusetts for religious reasons. He bought land from the Narragansett Native Americans and founded the city of Providence. He hoped to start a colony where people had religious and political freedom.

People seeking religious freedom soon followed Roger Williams into the Rhode Island area. Religious leader Anne Hutchinson and her followers founded the city of Portsmouth in 1638. Other communities sprang up shortly afterwards, including Newport, Warwick, Wickford, and Pawtuxet.

Eventually, the various communities united. In 1663, England's King Charles II granted them a royal charter, which created an official colony. The colonists were given more self-government than was offered to other American colonies at that time. This included the right to freedom of religion.

King Philip's War (1675-1676) arose from conflict between Native Americans and land-hungry white settlers. Many died, but the colonists eventually won. The Native Americans were also sickened by deadly diseases brought by Europeans. Thousands died because they had no natural resistance to illnesses such as smallpox and measles.

Colonists attack a Narragansett settlement during King Philip's War.

Rhode Islanders boarded and burned the British warship HMS Gaspee *in 1772.*

In the early 1700s, Rhode Island became very prosperous, thanks to farming and sea trading. Providence, Newport, and Bristol were bustling ports. Rhode Island also profited greatly from the African slave trade.

By the mid-1700s, the American colonies, including Rhode Island, had grown angry over unfair British taxes and laws. Most people wanted independence from Great Britain. In 1772, Rhode Islanders boarded a British warship called the HMS *Gaspee* and burned it. The incident resulted in more people calling for revolution.

During the Revolutionary War (1775-1783), British soldiers occupied Newport. Despite the loss of the city, many Rhode Islanders fought in the war's major battles.

After the war, Rhode Island became the last colony to ratify, or approve, the United States Constitution. It became the 13th state on May 29, 1790.

In the late 1700s, many factories were built in Rhode Island. New machines made it easier to mass produce goods such as textiles. This leap in manufacturing technology is known as the Industrial Revolution.

In 1793, North America's first water-powered cotton textile mill was built by Samuel Slater in Pawtucket, Rhode Island. In addition to textiles, other big industries in the state included jewelry and silverware.

Rhode Island prospered. Many people from Europe moved to the state to find jobs. Rich factory owners built huge mansions as summer homes in Newport. Many of the mansions are popular tourist destinations today.

In 1784, Rhode Island's legislature passed a law that eventually banned slavery. By the 1830s, thousands of runaway slaves fled the South. Many used the Underground Railroad in Rhode Island. It was a network of paths and safe houses where slaves could be sheltered and led to freedom.

Built in Pawtucket in 1793, Samuel Slater's mill was the first water-powered cotton textile mill in North America.

Civil War officers of the 1st Rhode Island Volunteers in 1861. The sign welcomes home their commander, Colonel Ambrose Burnside (center).

When the bloody Civil War (1861-1865) broke out, Rhode Island sent more than 25,000 troops to fight against the Southern Confederacy. The state's factories produced bullets, canons, firearms, and other materials that helped win the war for the North.

After the Civil War, Rhode Island's industry continued to grow. The state's factories produced goods such as cotton, wool, metal parts, and steam engines. In the first half of the 20th century, Rhode Island produced many supplies for America's involvement in World War I (1914-1918) and World War II (1939-1945).

Today, Rhode Island doesn't depend so much on manufacturing. Tourism and other service industries, such as health care, are the state's leading employers.

DID YOU KNOW?

Rhode Island and Providence Plantations

• Rhode Island is the smallest state in the Union, yet it has the longest official name: Rhode Island and Providence Plantations. It received that name in 1663 when King Charles II of England granted the royal charter making it a colony. The charter bound together the settlements of Warwick and Providence, which was referred to as Providence Plantations. Some people object to the use of the term "plantations" in the state's name. They mistakenly believe it refers to the state's role in owning African slaves. However, the term was commonly used in the 1600s to mean people banding together to form a colony. In 2010, the people of Rhode Island voted whether to remove the word "plantations" from the state's official name. They overwhelmingly elected to keep the old name.

• Quahogs are Rhode Island's official state shellfish. These large clams are eaten all over New England, but in Rhode Island they are so popular there are annual quahog festivals celebrating the tasty shellfish. Quahogs are used in chowders and clam cakes. Especially treasured are "stuffies," in which the clam meat is chopped up and mixed with breadcrumbs, onions, herbs, peppers, and celery, and then stuffed back into the shell and baked. The word "quahog" comes from Narragansett Native Americans, who used the shellfish for food and decoration. Quahog is also the name of the fictional town in the popular animated television show *Family Guy*.

• Rhode Island has the world's biggest termite, named Nibbles Woodaway. The steel-and-fiberglass sculpture rests atop the Big Blue Bug Solutions building in Providence. Nibbles is 58 feet (18 m) long, 9 feet (2.7 m) high, and weighs 4,000 pounds (1,814 kg). It is 920 times bigger than a real termite.

PEOPLE

Nathanael Greene (1742-1786) was one of the most important and successful Continental Army generals during the Revolutionary War (1775-1783). He was George Washington's most trusted and dependable officer. He started the war as a militia private from Rhode Island. In 1775, after the siege of Boston, Massachusetts, he was promoted to the rank of brigadier general of the Continental Army. Greene and George Washington were the only two generals of the Continental Army who served throughout the entire war. Even when defeated, Greene inspired his troops, saying "We fight, get beaten, rise, and fight again." Greene was born on a farm near Warwick, Rhode Island.

Vinny Paz (1962-) is a five-time world championship boxer. Born Vincenzo Edward Pazienza, he won his first lightweight title fight in 1987, boxing under the nickname "The Pazmanian Devil." He won the junior middleweight crown in 1991. Shortly afterward, he broke his neck in a car accident. Doctors said he would never fight again, but Paz trained hard. He got back in the boxing ring and won more world titles. Paz was born in Cranston, Rhode Island.

Viola Davis (1965-) is a television, stage, and film actress. For her role as a maid in 2011's *The Help*, she won a Screen Actors Guild Award, and was nominated for a Golden Globe and Academy Award. In 2015, she became the first African American woman to win the Primetime Emmy Award for Outstanding Lead Actress in a Drama Series for her work in the television show *How to Get Away with Murder*. Davis grew up in Central Falls, Rhode Island.

H.P. Lovecraft (1890-1937) was a novelist and short story writer who told tales of horror and science fiction. His first success came in 1923 when *Weird Tales* magazine published some of his short stories. His most famous story was 1928's "The Call of Cthulhu." It is about an ancient, tentacle-headed monster from an undersea city. The story has terrified generations of eager readers. Lovecraft was born in Providence, Rhode Island.

Matthew C. Perry (1794-1858) was a commodore of the United States Navy. He served in the War of 1812 (1812-1815) and the Mexican-American War (1846-1848). He fought pirates in the Mediterranean Sea and the West Indies. He also helped the Navy convert its sailing ships to steam-powered vessels. In 1854, he negotiated a treaty with Japan that helped end that country's trade isolation. Perry was born in South Kingston, Rhode Island.

George M. Cohan (1878-1942) was a song composer, singer, actor, playwright, and stage play producer. He was involved in so many hit shows that he is often called "The Father of American Musical Comedy." A few of his most famous songs include "The Yankee Doodle Boy," "Give My Regards to Broadway," "Over There," and "You're a Grand Old Flag." Cohan was born in Providence, Rhode Island.

Meredith Vieira (1953-) is an Emmy Award-winning journalist and television show host. In the 1980s, she worked on two CBS news-magazine shows, *West 57th* and *60 Minutes*. At ABC, she was a co-host of *The View* from 1997-2006. From 2006-2011, she was a co-host for the NBC morning news program *Today*. She also hosted the game show *Who Wants to Be a Millionaire* from 2002-13. Vieira was born in Providence, Rhode Island.

CITIES

Providence is the capital of Rhode Island. It is also the state's largest city. Its population is about 179,207. It is located in the northeastern part of the state, where the Providence River empties into Narragansett Bay. Roger Williams founded Providence in 1636, making it one of the oldest cities in the United States. It grew into a major seaport and industrial center. Today, Providence is home to many companies in the service industry, including banks, hospitals, and schools. The city's biggest employer is Brown University. It enrolls more than 9,000 students. There are many parks and historic buildings in the city. The Rhode Island School of Design Museum has a collection of more than 91,000 works of art.

Newport is located on Aquidneck Island, where Narragansett Bay meets the Atlantic Ocean. Its population is about 24,232. It was once a major port city. Today, it is known as a summer resort city for New Englanders. It is famous for its many beautiful mansions built in the 1800s, as well as its many other historic buildings. Naval Station Newport is operated by the United States Navy. More than 17,000 officers are trained at the base, which is home to the Naval War College and the Naval Undersea Warfare Center. Nearly 6,000 people are employed at the base.

Pawtucket is in northeastern Rhode Island, just north of Providence. Its population is about 71,591. The city is hailed as the birthplace of the Industrial Revolution in America. Samuel Slater built North America's first water-powered cotton-spinning mill in Pawtucket in 1793. Other mills soon sprang up, turning the city into a manufacturing powerhouse. Today, most of the mills have shut down or moved away, but the city still has many manufacturers. Pawtucket's factories produce goods such as jewelry, silverware, textiles, and metal products. The city is also a big supporter of the arts.

Warwick Neck Lighthouse

Warwick is the second-largest city in Rhode Island. It is in the east-central part of the state, along the shores of Narragansett Bay. Founded in 1642, its population today is about 81,699. Its biggest employers are health care, telecommunications, insurance, government, and retail. There are many marinas, parks, and beaches in the city. Within Warwick is a historic village called Pontiac. It is the site of Pontiac Mills, which were built in 1863. They provided uniforms for Union soldiers in the Civil War, and made the original "Fruit of the Loom" textiles. The mills are now on the National Register of Historic Places.

TRANSPORTATION

There are 6,106 miles (9,827 km) of public roadways in Rhode Island. Interstate I-95 runs through the state from the southwest to the northeast, passing through Warwick, Providence, and Pawtucket.

There are more than 1,160 bridges in Rhode Island. The Claiborne Pell Bridge, commonly called the Newport Bridge, crosses Narragansett Bay. It connects the city of Newport on Aquidneck Island with the town of Jamestown on Conanicut Island. It is one of the longest suspension bridges in the world. It measures 1,600 feet (488 m) in length.

Claiborne Pell Bridge

The busiest commercial airport in the state is T.F. Green Airport in Warwick. It services about 5.5 million passengers yearly. There are also commercial airports in Westerly and Block Island.

Amtrak's Acela Express and Regional lines pass through Rhode Island. They link the state with large cities such as Boston, Massachusetts, and Washington, DC. The Acela Express whisks passengers along at speeds up to 150 miles per hour (241 kph). Freight trains in the state handle bulky goods such as chemicals, cement, and lumber.

The Port of Providence is New England's second-largest deepwater port. It handles millions of tons of cargo, including cement, fuel, salt, and scrap metal.

NATURAL
RESOURCES

There are 1,250 farms operating in Rhode Island. Most are small. The average farm size is 56 acres (23 ha). In total, farmland covers 70,000 acres (28,328 ha) of land. That is about 11 percent of the state's land area.

The most valuable crops raised in Rhode Island are hay, potatoes, corn for livestock, apples, and sweet corn. Other crops include berries, beans, melons, and peas. Many farmers earn income from greenhouse and nursery plants, or from growing Christmas trees. Top livestock animals are dairy cows, chickens, and hogs.

The Wicked Tulips Flower Farm in Johnston, Rhode Island, allows people to pick their own blooms.

Commercial fishing has long been an important industry for Rhode Island, although the business has declined in recent years. Top catches include cod, striped bass, bluefish, flounder, squid, haddock, whiting, oysters, and clams. Many lobsters were once caught off the state's Atlantic Ocean coast.

Commercial fishermen haul in a day's catch from the Atlantic Ocean.

However, today there are far fewer lobsters to be caught. Lobsters prefer cold water, but the Atlantic Ocean near Rhode Island has been warming. That means most lobsters are now found in waters farther north.

Forests cover 56 percent of Rhode Island's land area. About 2.8 million cubic feet (79,287 cubic m) of timber is harvested each year to make furniture, paper, and other wood products.

NATURAL RESOURCES

INDUSTRY

When Samuel Slater built the first water-powered cotton-spinning mill in Pawtucket in 1793, it started the American Industrial Revolution. Automation made it much easier to mass-produce goods such as textiles and machinery.

Today, Rhode Island's factories produce tools, jewelry, silverware, plastics, metal products, chemicals, and some textiles. Many well-known businesses operate in Rhode Island. They include Hasbro, the maker of toys and games such as Mr. Potato Head and Monopoly.

Hasbro Worldwide Headquarters is in Pawtucket, Rhode Island.

Tourists wait to take a harbor cruise at Newport, Rhode Island.

Rhode Island's economy today depends greatly on service industry jobs. The service industry represents about 60 percent of the state's employment. Instead of manufacturing products, service industries sell services to businesses and consumers. It includes businesses such as advertising, financial services, health care, insurance, restaurants, retail stores, law, marketing, and tourism.

In recent years, tourism has become a very large part of Rhode Island's economy. Visitors enjoy the state's historic sites and nearly 400 miles (644 km) of coastline. Tourists spend more than $5.75 billion yearly in the state, which adds more than 50,000 jobs. That means about 1 of every 10 Rhode Islanders is employed in the tourism industry.

INDUSTRY

SPORTS

Rhode Island's Pawtucket Red Sox are a Minor League Baseball team affiliated with the Boston Red Sox. They play home games at McCoy Stadium in Pawtucket. They have won several league and division championships. The Providence Bruins are an affiliate team of the National Hockey League's Boston Bruins. They won a Calder Cup championship in 1999, and have won several division titles. Other professional and semi-professional teams in the state represent rugby, baseball, soccer, and basketball.

The state has four colleges that compete in NCAA Division 1 games, the highest level of competition among colleges in the National Collegiate Athletic Association (NCAA). They include the Brown University Bears, the Bryant University Bulldogs, the Providence College Friars, and the University of Rhode Island Rams. The most-watched men's and women's sports played include football, basketball, ice hockey, baseball, tennis, soccer, and rugby. Rowing is also very popular.

With nearly 400 miles (644 km) of coastline, sailing has long been a favorite Rhode Island sport. The America's Cup yacht races were held at Newport for more than 50 years, from 1930 to 1983.

America's Cup Challenger Series competitors sail off Newport, Rhode Island, in June 2012.

ENTERTAINMENT

Rhode Islanders have many wonderful festivals, fairs, and museums to choose from. The Newport Jazz Festival has featured world-class musicians since 1954, including superstars such as Norah Jones, Kamasi Washington, and Chick Corea. The three-day festival draws thousands of jazz lovers to Newport's Fort Adams State Park, overlooking Narragansett Bay.

The ocean is a big part of Rhode Island life, so it's no surprise that there are many excellent sailing-related museums in the state. The Herreshoff Marine Museum and America's Cup Hall of Fame is in Bristol. Located along the shores of Narragansett Bay, it restores and preserves dozens of maritime treasures, including vessels from the 1800s. The Naval War College Museum, in Newport, is operated by the United States Navy. Its exhibits highlight Narragansett Bay and the history of the Navy in the region.

Newport Jazz Festival

Newport's International Tennis Hall of Fame Museum features photographs, videos, audio recordings, trophies, art, and tennis equipment and apparel, from the sport's historical beginnings to the modern era.

The International Tennis Hall of Fame Museum is in Newport. The museum's collections include more than 1,900 artifacts and photos that tell the history of the "sport of kings." The first U.S. National Championship tennis tournament took place in Newport in 1881.

The Roger Williams Park Zoo is in Providence. Founded in 1872, it is one of the oldest zoos in the country. The zoo is home to more than 100 species of animals, including giraffes, elephants, bison, and zebras.

TIMELINE

6,000-8,000 BC—The first Paleo-Indians arrive in the Rhode Island area.

1500s—Native American tribes establish themselves in the Rhode Island area, including the Wampanoag, Pequot, Narraganset, and Nipmuck people.

1524—Italian explorer Giovanni de Verrazzano reaches Rhode Island.

1614—Dutch sailor Adriaen Block explores the Rhode Island area.

1636—Roger Williams founds the city of Providence, the first permanent European settlement in Rhode Island.

1663—Rhode Island becomes an English colony.

1675-1676—King Philip's War is fought. Many colonists and Native Americans die before the colonists win.

1772—Anger over unfair British taxes and laws boils over when Rhode Islanders burn the British ship HMS *Gaspee* in Narragansett Bay.

1784—Rhode Island's legislature passes a law that eventually bans slavery.

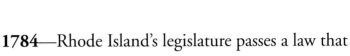

1790—Rhode Island ratifies the United States Constitution and becomes the 13th state.

1793—First water-powered cotton textile mill is built by Samuel Slater.

1861-1865—More than 25,000 Rhode Islanders serve in the Civil War. Rhode Island stays in the Union, fighting against the Southern Confederacy.

1881—First U.S. National Championship tennis tournament held in Newport, Rhode Island.

1930-1983—The America's Cup yacht race is held off the shores of Newport.

2015—The Providence Friars men's ice hockey team wins the NCAA national championship.

GLOSSARY

America's Cup

The most prestigious trophy awarded in the sport of sailing. It attracts top sailors and yacht designers. Sailors have competed for the America's Cup since 1851.

Estuary

The mouth of a freshwater river, where it meets the sea and mixes with saltwater. Estuaries mark the transition zone between river and ocean ecosystems. Many kinds of unique plants and animals live in estuaries.

Glacier

A huge, slow-moving sheet of ice that grows and shrinks as the climate changes. The ice sheets can be more than one mile (1.6 km) thick.

Industrial Revolution

Advances in machine technology, especially in steam power, iron-making, and textiles. During the Industrial Revolution, the world's economies started relying more on manufacturing instead of farming and manual labor.

Moraine

A large pile of silt and other debris left by a glacier. The deposits usually make good farmland.

New England

An area in the northeast United States. It consists of the states of Connecticut, Maine, Massachusetts, New Hampshire, Vermont, and Rhode Island.

PURITAN

A religious group of the 16th and 17th centuries. They were English Protestants who wanted to "purify" the Church of England. They could be very strict in how they practiced Christianity. Many left England to seek religious freedom in North America.

REVOLUTIONARY WAR

The war fought between the American colonies and Great Britain from 1775-1783. It is also known as the War of Independence or the American Revolution.

SMALLPOX

An often-deadly disease caused by a virus and unknowingly brought by Europeans to the Americas. Symptoms of smallpox include a high fever followed by a body rash. Smallpox epidemics frequently killed thousands of native peoples who had no immunity to the disease. Today, smallpox vaccines have eliminated outbreaks of the disease.

STORM SURGE

When hurricane winds push the ocean's water onto land. The rise in the water level can flood low-lying islands, cities, and farms. Storm surges can be deadly.

UNDERGROUND RAILROAD

In the early to mid-1800s, people created the Underground Railroad to help African Americans escape from slave states. Not an actual railroad, it was instead a secret network of safe houses and connecting routes that led slaves to freedom.

INDEX